A Beginner's Guide to Meditation

Your Path to Wisdom

Duangta Wanthong Mondi

Published by Red Dragon Publishing

A Beginner's Guide to Meditation

http://www.teachermondi.com

Copyright © 2015 Red Dragon Publishing, London

Edited by Russ Crowley, Red Dragon Publishing

ISBN: 978-1-908203-18-2
ISBN: 978-1514784730 (CreateSpace-assigned ISBN)

Why You Should Read This Book

This short beginner's guide to meditation will help you learn and about meditation, why you should do it, how you do it, the benefits that can be obtained, and how it will improve your life.

Meditation is something that you can practice almost anywhere and, as the benefits are both tangible and can be experienced in a very short time, you will rapidly reap the rewards of regular practice. Though predominantly an Eastern practice, the benefits of meditation are assisting in the spread throughout the Western world and many are beginning to realize that, in the ever-increasing stresses of daily life, something more is needed. Meditation can fulfil that need.

About The Author

Duangta Wanthong Mondi is Thai and a Buddhist. She grew up and lives in a rural area in North-east of Thailand, where she works as an English teacher in a Thai State school. Duangta's family are Buddhists, and meditation has been a part of her life since a very young age.

For more about the author and her books, refer to page 51.

Preface

I first started to practice meditation when I was 7 years old. My family are Buddhists and I always went with my grandmother to the temple. Every Buddhist holy day, my grandmother would go there early in the morning, take the required 8 precepts, and practice meditation. She would stay at the temple overnight and, when she departed the following morning, would leave the 8 precepts behind, take the 5 precepts for normal life, and then go home. She did this 4 times a month, on holy days, for her entire life.

My own first experience of meditating was when the temple hosted a ten day meditation camp for monks, nuns, and Buddhists. Just a little girl, I took the 8 precepts and then was expected to perform the same as the adults: we woke up at 3:30 in the morning and I washed myself. At 4 a.m., we were ready for the day and all chanted for an hour. We then meditated from 5 to 6. Following which we had breakfast— the first of the day's two meals. We were then permitted 2 hours to relax, and then we practiced meditation until lunch at 11. The practice started again from 1 to 4 p.m., followed by washing and having soft drinks (in place of dinner). At 6 p.m., we all chanted again for an hour, before the final hour of meditation. We all then went to sleep at 9 p.m.

At the time, even though I didn't understand that much about the purpose of meditating, I knew I enjoyed it. Later, I discovered what meditation gives you, and I've since been looking for how to improve my ability, how to reach the goal of meditation, as well as how to achieve it without hurting my body. This book is useful for anyone who wants to start practicing meditation in a correct manner, and has been written from my own meditation experiences.

My book, A Beginner's Guide to Meditation, will help you in getting started with meditation both successfully and in a short time. You will then see how meditation can and will improve your life in many ways. Of course, to do this you must try it yourself to appreciate what I write about, to see what I mean, to sense what I feel, and to achieve what I have—the true happiness.

Also, dedicated to you.

Table of Contents

Table of Figures

"The mind can go in a thousand directions, but on this beautiful path, I walk in peace. With each step, the wind blows. With each step, a flower blooms."

Thích Nhất Hạnh

Figure 1 - The Author

1

Getting Ready for Meditation

Preparing for Meditation

There are few things that you have to consider before starting your meditation exercise, but these are essential towards the success of your exercise practice; so it's a good idea to ensure that these are correct.

- Clothing

  Comfortable and appropriate clothing can make all the difference when planning for meditation. You want to be wearing something which is both loose and allows you to easily relax in. Perhaps you've seen pictures of people meditating before, and noticed that many of them wearing a plain, light, and loose cotton outfit—this is selected for a reason: it's complete, it's comfortable, and it helps you settle nicely into the mood. Conversely, if your shirt is too tight, or your pants are too rough on your skin, then they're going to quickly distract you, and prevent you from achieving what you set out to do. Your clothes are the first step towards framing your mind for meditation, moving towards the desired focus, and gaining the level of energy required. Indeed, obtaining the right clothing will make peace and contentment much easier to attain.

Figure 2 – Wear Comfortable Clothing

- Breathing

It might sound a little strange, but breathing is the next step in preparing for your meditation. Slow, regular breathing is the key to settling your mind and starting your meditation, so try and establish a breathing pattern as soon as you can. If you can do this before you begin meditation, you may find the practice much easier. For beginners, the basic breathing technique refers to simple inhales and exhales, such as when you're sitting relaxed or even asleep.

When you breathe, try to remain still and feel the sensations of your breathing in your chest and abdomen, as they swell and rise on the inward breath, and collapse and fall on the outward breath. While practicing your breathing, try your best to eliminate all the thoughts in your mind, as this is both the key to effective meditation and, with all the distractions, noises around you, one of the most challenging. So, as you focus only on your breathing, as you first inhale you sense mentally the air passing in through your nose; then, as you exhale gently through slightly parted lips, you feel this slow expulsion of air in your mind also. Next, repeat the process again and again until your body naturally conforms to the process.

When you're ready to dig deeper into your relaxation, make a conscious switch with your breathing by taking slow, deep breaths, counting slowly to 3 as you inhale...1, 2, 3 and then letting the air slowly out to the same count as you exhale... 1, 2, 3. As you improve, you may find you can increase the inhale/exhale rate, to 5, 7, etc. Repeat this slow breathing process to boost the supply of oxygen that is needed to further relax your thoughts. Thankfully, you can practice your breathing anywhere and anytime it suits you.

- Place and Time

  There is no recommended time or place for meditation because it all depends on the individual and their choices. Generally, the best place to perform your daily meditation would be a pleasant, quiet, and comfortable area free from disturbances and distractions. However, before you think of meditating in bed, doing the practice in there is not advisable as there's a high risk of falling into sleep after a few minutes or so. When you do find a suitable place, you should try and ensure that you can use the same place at the same time every day (as stressing out looking for your next meditation venue isn't great for a focused mind).

  Though the ideal time for meditation is between 3 and 4 a.m., this is not practical for many folk due to scheduling conflicts and a myriad of other reasons. So, the next best time is either early morning or late at night; but again, it depends on your time, availability, and preference; and is something that you should identify as the best time for your own meditation.

Sitting Meditation

Because its primary purpose is to relax your thoughts and lessen the amount of unnecessary mind activity required to achieve a certain level of consciousness, sitting meditation doesn't require any complicated techniques: you practice sitting meditation with your eyes closed.

Figure 3 – Hands in Lap, Thumbs Touching, Feet Flat

Figure 4 - Hands in Lap, Thumbs Touching, Foot on Thigh

Figure 5 - Hands on Knee Thumbs Touching, Feet Flat

Figure 6 - Hands on Knee Thumbs Touching, Foot on Thigh

Ideally, it is done by sitting on the ground, on a meditation mat, or cushion to alleviate any strain on your body. However, not everyone is comfortable in this position, so meditating while sitting on a chair is acceptable as long as the body isn't leaning back and being supported.

- Posture

  Sit up straight and don't lean back. It is important to make sure that you alone are supporting your upper body. Tilt your pelvis forward slightly to push your butt backwards and your abdomen forwards. This posture will automatically and naturally arch your lower back, and help your body to relax.

- Legs

  There are two different options for positioning your legs:

  o Sitting in a crossed-leg position with one foot on top of the opposite thigh, while the other one rests underneath the opposing leg (refer to Figure 3).

  o Sitting in a crossed-leg position with your feet resting on top of your thighs (refer to Figure 4).

- Hands

  There are also two different options for the positions of your hands:

  a. Hold your hands in front of you and with the tips of the fingers and thumb of your left hand, against those of the right to form an oval. This process will help maintain and circulate the same level of energy through your body (refer to Figure 3 and Figure 4).

b. Place your right hand flat in the palm of your left hand and then place your thumb tips together (refer to Figure 5 and Figure 6).

Walking Meditation

Although many people associate meditation with a sitting position, walking meditation is actually a lot easier for some because they can both feel the intense energy of their own movements while also achieving the required level of consciousness. To compare, with the walking method you can focus and meditate as you use your muscles; whereas with the sitting method there is a high risk of falling asleep or getting distracted by different thoughts and anxieties running through your mind.

Naturally, meditation while walking has different requirements: for safety's sake, your eyes must be open while performing this practice; and you should try and feel your body's movements as part of the art of concentration.

In walking meditation, you do not divert your thoughts or attention outside of the real world because you need to be alert and consider the elements and environment around you while practicing. For instance, though you do have to concentrate on your inner energy, you must also ensure you don't trip or fall down a hole.

- Posture

  Stand up straight and, to help prepare your body to obtain focus, ensure your neck and back are straight. Slouching may bring on negative effects, such as making it difficult to find your level of consciousness.

- Legs

  Stand on flat feet and bend your knees a little to help your blood circulation, and energy flow throughout your body.

Figure 7 - Walking Meditation Posture

- Chest

  Drop your shoulders and cave your chest slightly to release all tension from your upper body. This way, it's easier to calm your breathing, and to maintain a steady supply of oxygen while you walk.

- Hands

  For most practitioners, you maintain and circulate your level of energy by placing the tips of the thumb and forefinger together on each hand. However, if preferred, another position is where you can place your hands down by your side while walking. Furthermore, others have also suggested that placing your hands behind your lower back, with the right hand holding the wrist of the left hand, is also a good position (**Note**: this is the author's preferred hand position for walking meditation).

Figure 8 - The Author and Her Preferred Hand Position for Standing Meditation

Knowing Your Mind

Our mind is the initiator of the things that we experience in our lives. As such, every one of us should take positive steps to understand the nature of our own mind; and, regardless of whether our mind is filled with good or bad thoughts, be aware that our thoughts are powerful enough to take control of any situation. There needs to be an element of caution here, as if you are not strong or cautious enough, it can lead you to a worsening condition.

We will now look at our mind's make-up.

Ordinary Mind vs. Innermost Essence

The nature of our mind is divided into 2 parts: the ordinary mind and the inner mind. The ordinary mind (*Sem*), is the promoter of negative thoughts in our lives, those stimulators of hatred and ill feelings, and the agent that loses hope and causes weariness. An ordinary mind sees the situation as it is in the outside world— hopeless and irrevocable; and looks for the destruction of great ideas and conscience. Furthermore, Sem is also the nature of the mind that conceals the existence of the innermost essence of the second part of the human mind—the inner mind.

The inner mind (*Rigpa*) contains both wisdom and awareness and allows our subconscious to understand and appreciate everything. With Rigpa, we can look at all the positive perspectives of life in the midst of all the worries, undesirable events and attitudes that are present; and, not only will we be aware of them, but we can also address them in a calm and rational manner. Unfortunately, Sem is able to obscure this particular state of awareness, thereby increasing anxiety and other negative thoughts and emotions, which hinder our path to achieving our goals.

It is clear to see that Rigpa is the mental state that we are trying to open up and develop when we meditate: in doing so, we look forward to achieving positive thought which, when perfected, will overcome and conquer all hindrances.

Take a few moments to evaluate your own mind now, and to determine which of these natures of mind is most prominent now. It may be a bit confusing to actually take control of your mind when you believe it to be in an ordinary state; however, healthy, stress free thoughts are choices which we should all consider as being more powerful and more welcome than those filled with uncertainties, doubts, and fears.

In Buddhism, everything is circular—there is cause and there is effect; and, the mind is no different—our internal thoughts and feelings affect our lives. As we well know, our 'inner life' is influenced by events around us, which in turn affects our reaction to these events—our behavior. This reaction again changes what is going on around us, and affects our inner life again—it is a circular process. The mind is also said to affect our karma. Karma is how our deliberate actions lead to future consequences in our lives—again, cause and effect. Moreover, our deliberate thoughts and our inner life can also affect this: negative inner thoughts can create negative energy in much the same way as negative actions.

We only have to look at babies to know that our minds are essentially pure, and negative or distracting thoughts like hate and worry enter into our mind from outside—they are not things we are born with. However, it is encouraging to know that this negativity can be removed through meditation and attention to our spirituality: meditation purifies the mind, liberating it from earthly things that muddle and confuse it, allowing the meditator to feel both cleansed and free.

In Tibetan Buddhism, the mind has three inseparable elements: perceptions, projections, and phenomena. The mind perceives things around us through the use of our senses: nothing around us exists without us perceiving it. We then project our own thoughts onto these items, and assign them labels so our brains can readily organize them. Once labelled, concepts such as our sense of self become phenomena that we then project onto our perceptions— once again, it is circular. Essentially, humans are nothing more than a product of our own physical and psychological processes.

Enlightenment occurs when one can observe their own perceptions and know that they are of the mind, and they are insubstantial. The enlightened individual observes these phenomena and lets them go. Consequently, earthly emotions like anger, excitement, and fear have no effect, because an enlightened person sees them for what they are—perceptions. They are also able to see their dreams in the same way, and to change them as required. As I hope you can see, when one has this flexibility of mind it enhances their ability to control emotions, desires, etc.

Buddhism also emphasizes that there are different levels and categories of the mind, including: a waking state, a dreaming state, and a state of enlightenment. However, there are also many more subconscious levels of the mind that are imperceptible to us. In addition, there is also the concept of the primary mind, which processes things as a whole; and the secondary mind, which processes the details. As we can see, the mind itself is a layered and multifaceted entity, and by being aware of its complexities, meditation can help us access those deeper layers and help us to control our thoughts in an extremely beneficial manner.

Another important step to understanding the nature of the mind is to understand the three marks of existence: inadequacy, impermanence, and existence/not-self. The first mark is inadequacy: one of the major goals of a traditional Buddhist is to eradicate their sense of incompetence and insufficiency, and dispel negative emotions, such as frustration and sadness, as well as physical sensations, such as pain. The second mark is impermanence: the awareness that we are just a temporary entity and are just passing through this life on this Earth—we will die. The final mark of existence is the idea of our actual existence/our 'not-self': this can be difficult to grasp for many people new to Buddhism or meditation, but the basis of this concept is that our consciousness and sensations are not ourselves; and therefore, our true selves transcend these.

Of course, there are many more complex details to the Buddhist interpretation of the mind, but these are the ones most related to meditation; and, understanding these ideas can be extremely beneficial to those starting to practice meditation.

Bring Your Mind to the Present

One of the most important aspects of meditation in the modern world is bringing your mind to the present moment—the here and now. It is both extremely tempting and easy to dwell on things that have happened in the past, or to focus so much on your goals and worries for the future, that you actually miss what is happening in the present.

Bringing your mind to the present is mainly an exercise in concentration and focus, and is why meditation is such an extremely effective way of helping with this. Meditating will empty your mind of all concerns that are not relevant to the now, the present moment. So, from this point onwards, try to apply the principle of observing events around you and letting them go from your life. If something negative or stressful is happening, just ignore it: don't start to worry about all the horrible things that could come out of it as this just generates negative energy and pulls you out of the present moment. Instead, take a few deep breaths, and continue to focus on the present to improve the situation.

It is also extremely important to focus on the positive sides of your present situation as much as possible, no matter how small they are. Take a few minutes each day to enjoy something that makes you happy: maybe it's reading a chapter of your favorite book, or taking a walk in your favorite park. While you are there, stay in the moment and enjoy these things, it will boost your positive energy and make you more active and cheerful. Another thing that is important is to assess all you are thankful for whenever you start to feel pessimistic, angry, or sad about something. Even if they are small things, this is a great reminder that there is good in the world—in your world—and that you are lucky to be a part of it.

Something else that is very difficult to do when it comes to staying in the present is to successfully work towards your goals. You are probably wondering how to make any sort of progress if you avoid thinking about the future. The answer here is to set a series of steps towards your goal, and then immerse yourself in the first step. Don't try and think about the next step, or the previous step if you're further from your goal, just focus on the current one. Try to detach yourself from your end result, because though important, it can be detrimental to your current work if you're focused on it too much. Allocating all of your focus to your daily activities is much more productive.

This level of focus can also even improve your intelligence. You see, when we aren't living in the present moment, it is hard for us to access the full extent of our knowledge and the things that we have learned. But when we clear our minds, truly live in the present, and focus on the task at hand, it is incredible what our brains can do. Therefore, not only can meditation improve performance, but studies have shown that it improves cognition, memory, and even test-taking ability.

Key to remaining present is to work on minimizing the number of self-related distracting thoughts you process throughout your day. Often, when we are struggling with something, we are actually our own worst enemy. When we are faltering it's often because our thoughts are turned inwards ('in our own heads'), instead of thinking about the current problem. For example, instead of concentrating on what your peers are saying during a work meeting, you're thinking about your own problems: about the argument you had at home last night, or all the emails that are mounting up. Focus here is crucial, both during meditation practice and throughout the day; and, you will discover that incorporating the Buddhist principle of 'no-self' into your own life is very beneficial.

Banish Negativity and Be Happy

One of the biggest ways meditation can affect your life is to rid it of negative energy. By ridding yourself of this negativity, you will immediately feel more positive (cause and effect). This might sound like a bit of a con, but it isn't: quite simply, if you remove a weight from something, the load is less. A common goal is to find true happiness amidst who you are, and meditation is a great way to do this. That is also why meditation is often recommended as a way to cope with mental health issues such as depression and anxiety. While general breath-based meditation will naturally improve your mood over time, meditation performed with specific focus on positivity will make an incredible difference to your well-being.

Whenever you meditate, take time to think about the positive things in your life and really notice them for what they are. It is often difficult for us to notice positive things when we are stressed, because they are so easy to take for granted. So, notice the positive things around you, and in your life; and think about how you are going to carry them with you throughout your day so they are there when you need them. If you subsequently find yourself in a situation where you start to get stressed, think of one of your positives. Over time, you will then associate this positivity with calm, and you'll be able to handle stressful situations much better and with a more optimistic outlook.

Another great benefit to becoming more positive is that it will attract other positive individuals. Maintaining a positive environment is a sure-fire and great way to stay happy; and, if you are a force of positivity, it may also help others around you who may be struggling with their own stress or emotions.

Of course, staying positive is much easier said than done, but it is important to keep working at it, even when it does get difficult. Try to make meditation and positive thinking a habit as soon as you can. Even if you are having a hard time staying positive, or you forget to meditate one day, just start again tomorrow and keep trying. Eventually, it will become much easier. Also, take notice of yourself, and if you find yourself slipping into a rut of negativity, analyze what's happening to see if you can try to break that cycle. When you're fixated on something negative, it is easy to start noticing all the other negative things in your life (no matter how small), which will only lead to further frustration and stress— focusing on staying calm is crucial.

Meditation can also be used to improve many different elements of your life: from physical healing to job performance, and from increased focus to greater productivity, there are so many benefits to daily meditation practice. With a little focus and dedication, anyone can make meditation a part of their routine and reap a multitude of benefits.

Benefits of Meditation

As we've already covered, there are both physical and mental benefits to be found through meditation, including mind control, inner peace, and great wisdom. In fact, each individual will have different reasons for engaging in this practice, but what is important is that you start practicing as soon as you can because these positive effects are only attainable if done regularly.

Mind Control

Though these two words are often associated with telekinesis or some other supernatural power, mind control in meditation refers to your ability to manage all the distractions around you. Our world is filled with negative thoughts and realities, such as sadness, depression, anxiety, fear and doubt; and meditation helps to develop your mind towards the highest level of control. In fact, when you become proficient enough, you can transform all your negative energy into positive energy with your mind.

Inner Peace

Peace or tranquillity is a state of mind where a person is totally free from any form of anxiety. Having already read this far, you can see now how this can be achieved by meditation; and, as inner peace comes from within you and your senses—a supreme contentment that is just there, deep inside of you—the kind of harmony you will receive here is different from that offered by the material world.

Great Wisdom

As you may know, knowledge and wisdom are entirely different. Knowledge is a skill which can be developed and achieved by studying hard, but it often takes years of practice, enormous mental effort, as well as a desire and willingness to learn. In contrast, wisdom is more of a special gift of intuition and fair judgement that is present in different forms, i.e. sensitive instincts, hereditary factors, mental capability and breeding.

Meditation offers wisdom to an advanced level of thinking, and can make situations far clearer and easier to understand. It makes learning and comprehending many wonders of life much simpler, even if the clues themselves are difficult to explain.

Uses of Meditation in Your Life

Mind relaxation also brings two important advantages to our everyday lives, which should never be taken for granted: healing and performance enhancement.

Healing

One of the biggest benefits of meditation is in its healing powers. Opening the mind by meditation, and the stability this offers, is ideal for allowing the body to repair itself. Meditation can help us both physically and mentally: physically, by allowing our minds to recover from the exhaustions of daily life, and mentally by either improving the symptoms of an existing mental condition, or by decreasing the chances of one ever occurring.

Meditation has a number of mental and emotional advantages, and there is scientific basis that also shows there are a number of medical advantages and remedies to different types of body illnesses.

A Harvard Medical School research comparing those who performed meditation practices for a significant period of time versus those who didn't, showed that those who did practice developed a "disease fighting gene".

According to author Jay Winner, stress is the major cause of a variety of illnesses. In fact, people who suffer with negativity and stress often develop health issues, ranging from simple to serious. Some examples of afflictions caused by stress are constipation, headache, ulcers, muscle and joint problems, high blood pressure, cancers, etc.

If you feel stressed, you know you need to relax—relaxation opposes stress. Therefore, if your mind is relaxed and at peace, the systems in your body are functioning normally and correctly, and will both prevent and fight the toxins inside of you. Moreover, scientific studies have confirmed the positive benefits of meditation. John L. Craven, found that meditation consistently reduced symptoms of stress-related conditions. This applied mainly to anxiety, but also to a number of other conditions, including chronic pain, hypertension, and asthma.

Meditation is also helpful for easing symptoms of chronic physical illnesses or problems. Our body's resistance to disease and pain drops when we are stressed and, due to our brain's 'fight or flight' response, this creates adrenaline. When this occurs, the body's repairing mechanisms—the ones that generate new cells and create antibodies to fight off infection—cannot work efficiently, thereby increasing the risk of sickness.

Additionally, meditation benefits many conditions unrelated to stress. Studies by Harvard professor, Herbert Benson, indicates that meditation can improve symptoms of serious diseases, such as cancer and AIDS, as well as assist with coughing, nausea, general tension, and pain throughout the entire body. The relaxed state of meditation allows the body to release tension stored throughout our busy workdays, and offers much needed pain relief. Likewise, it can also help reduce our respiratory system and our heart rate, as well as reducing stress-based cortisol in the brain.

Furthermore, the deep breathing associated with meditation is especially helpful, because the oxygen you are receiving is a life support for your body functions, and the relaxing rhythm of this deep breathing will further decrease the amount of tension that you feel.

Earlier, we mentioned the healing benefits of meditation for troubled mental or emotional states. Nowadays, with ever busier and hectic lives, it's almost as if we are in constant worry about our everyday problems; and, it is therefore important that we create a positive state of mind to help manage this—meditation can help us achieve this state.

Meditation can assist us in viewing our problems in a different light; and, by observing them calmly, instead of feeling stressed and irritable, you will be able to manage them and let them go. Moreover, by helping to release the negative energy, thoughts, and tension that the person has been carrying around with them, meditation can also help struggles with emotional trauma or past stressful events, allowing the person to move forward with positivity and calm.

The spiritual element of meditation can also be extremely helpful for many people. You see, when the focus is on spirituality, meditation can engender a feeling of a sense of connection with something greater than themselves. This can create a much more positive outlook in the meditator, reduce stress, and make them happier. It also helps the meditator to feel closer to, and connected with, the natural world. This itself can help improve strength, reduce muscle tension, and reduce instances of the 'placebo effect' (where, by expecting to have a certain symptom, a person then creates that symptom).

To summarize, the healing powers of meditation are actually quite formidable and can benefit sufferers of many different conditions.

Enhancing your performance

Meditation can also be used to enhance performance in many aspects of our lives: at work, in physical areas, such as athletics, and even with our social lives. Indeed, dedicated focus for just a few minutes a day can drastically improve the quality of life for many people.

If you are stressed, your mental and physiological ability suffer. That is why there's a great chance that you'll perform poorly in the office or at home. Being stressed means your ability to think clearly and your response to certain situations can become dull and incoherent.

As a result, many successful professionals use regular meditation to keep them composed and focused throughout what would otherwise be stressful lives. This composure, in turn, helps increase their professional successes. For example, meditating before going to work each morning will help you stay present during the workday, which could lead you to increased idea generation and better decision making. It can also increase your enjoyment of your work because, by focus on the positives, the stress and negative aspects of the job that were present before no longer weigh you down. The knock-on effect of this is your personal environment changes and others will become attracted to you and want to work with you. It may also make it easier to take professional risks without the normally associated extra anxiety that comes with it.

Again, we touched on this before, one of the most important points when meditating to improve job success is to stay focused on the present and remain in the moment (this applies to any area though, not just performance enhancement). While it is great to have goals and to know what you want out of your career, it is much easier to achieve those goals if you are successful in the present moment and invest yourself in the projects you are currently working on. Also, if you ever find yourself in a stressful situation at work, it will help to meditate. Take a few minutes in your office to just close your eyes and focus on your breathing. This will keep you from being overwhelmed by the situation and allow you to remain calm.

Naturally, meditation is also a great tool for athletes looking to improve their performance. While working physically towards your athletic goals is obviously very important, it is hard to make progress without a strong, clear and determined mind. However, a few minutes of quiet meditation that allows you to clear your mind and focus on your breath will not only release tension that may be negatively affecting your performance, but can also empty your mind of any self-doubt that may stand in the way. Take time to notice the things that are happening around you and then let them go. Once you have done that you can use visualization—where you picture yourself achieving your athletic goals easily and with perfect form—as many times and as often as you want.

Indeed, positive visualization has been proven to improve athletic performance. Studies in Psychology Today and The Journal of Sport & Exercise Psychology have shown that visualization activates the neurons that control the muscles that perform the exercise without physically doing it: the brain is essentially training without exerting any physical effort—this is a technique used by many Olympic athletes.

As meditation increases activity in the cortex of the brain, this helps us process emotions more efficiently and makes us feel happier. By doing so, it also decreases the feelings of fear and stress that are associated with socializing, and can thereby improve our social lives. This is especially beneficial to those struggling with communal anxiety, as removing these negative feelings makes us more willing to participate in the community. As you probably know, feeling happier can affect your social life in many positive ways, especially in attracting others closer to you.

If you practice regularly, meditation also offers improvements to your mental and emotional stability, including enhancing creativity and focus, increasing peace-of-mind, decreasing worries and anxiety, and removing uncertainties. As can be seen, meditation can bring many advantages to your performance enhancement, not least of which is equipping you with the necessary tools to manage and conquer any given situation confidently and calmly.

2

Basic Knowledge about Meditation

In this chapter, we will first look at the basic knowledge of meditation; and second, we will distinguish between the terms concentration and meditation.

Concentration

Focusing your mind on a particular subject involves a process called Concentration (*Samadhi*). The word concentrate refers to an exclusive mental application where your mind is focused on a particular subject or object to then develop your thoughts. Concentration requires both will and energy to attain the required level; and, as this can be demanding, often leads to exhaustion if done incorrectly. Mental involvement is often one of the major factors required to attain any goal; and, though concentration means focusing internally, it must still keep you aware of your outside world. This enables you to think clearly about a subject, enables you to become involved with that topic, and may even enable you to solve or manage it. The purpose of being in this state of mind is to be able to gain control over something by using your mind's energy, while simultaneously ignoring everything else that may distract you.

Levels of Concentration

While practicing concentration, you will experience different thoughts and feelings in your mind, depending on how much focus there currently is in your mind: there are three levels of concentration, called The Threefold Concentration, and these are: momentary concentration, access concentration, and absorption concentration.

Momentary Concentration

Momentary concentration (*Kanika Samadhi*), is the preliminary stage towards achieving the supreme stage, or completely fixed concentration. At this stage, your level of focus is already determined, but your thoughts will likely jump about from one subject to another without any break in your mind's energy. This doesn't mean that your concentration is inconsistent or weak, it's just the focal point of your mind is turning its attention elsewhere. A person in this stage can both be aware of their inner and outer environment and, even though they are drawn by distractions, if the person has the capability to do so, it is still possible to sustain this energy.

Access Concentration

Access concentration (*Upacara Samadhi*) or neighborhood concentration is a powerful and more enhanced level than momentary concentration. At this second level, the person's mind is fixed on only one object, and does not falter by distractions. A person at this level has great control on their mind, so even if a weak element which may compromise the level of concentration arises, the possibility that the practitioner may gain access to the 3rd level of deeper concentration is still attainable. While at this level, you must be cautious about control of your concentration as it is easy to doze off if not properly handled or unaware.

Absorption Concentration

Absorption concentration (*Appana Samadhi*) is the highest form and most intensive of The Threefold Concentration. People at this level have mastered the first and second levels of concentration and become too engrossed with a subject to ever be distracted. A person who has achieved this level appears more than asleep because their focus is not present in the outer world.

Now we will look at meditation.

Meditation

Meditation is a technique used to develop your consciousness and to train your mind to indulge in clear thoughts without becoming sidetracked or distracted. Unlike concentration, the main purposes of meditation are to find tranquility and inner peace while clearing out all negativity and worries from inside your head. Whether you are experiencing negative or positive thoughts—hindrances— all you need do is calm your senses and obtain peace to achieve meditative absorption. However, for beginners, obtaining peace, or ignoring hindrances, is one of the hardest tasks.

When we meditate, we can gauge our 'level of meditation' (the level we, as an individual are at) in a number of ways; one way is by comparing it against the 4 levels of meditative absorption: in Sanskrit, this is called Jhana (*Dhyana*), and it is a sequence of refined states of mind which leads to impeccable composure and cognizance. We will come onto what this actually is shortly, but the way we gauge this is looking at what hindrances still affect us.

The Five Hindrances

As your proficiency with meditation increases, you will eliminate the following five hindrances to progress through the absorption levels: sensory desire, ill will, sloth and torpor, restlessness and worry, doubt.

We will look at each of these in greater detail in the next chapter, but for now it's good to know that they exist. We will now look at defining the meditative absorption factors.

The Five Meditative Absorption Factors

As mentioned just now, there are 4 meditative absorption levels, the sequence of refined states of mind which leads to impeccable composure and cognizance.

These are inextricably linked to the five factors of meditative absorption. These are: 1) applied thinking, 2) sustained thinking, 3) rapture, 4) bliss, and 5) one-pointedness. In the same way that you must eliminate the five hindrances to progress through the meditative absorption levels, you must also master these factors before you can advance to the next level of absorption—hindrances, meditative absorption factors, and meditative absorption levels are all interlinked.

1. Applied thinking

   The very first factor is applied thinking (*Vitakka*). This is the process of steadying your consciousness onto the theme of meditation, and what you are trying to achieve. Doing so will assist the mind in firmly holding its focus on the desired object.

2. Sustained thinking

   The second factor is sustained thinking (*Vicara*), and its primary function is to sustain and maintain the level of energy achieved during level 1. Your consciousness is already in its meditative state, and sustained thinking will take control allowing you to progress and move to the next level.

3. Rapture

   The next factor is called rapture (*Piti*), and is defined as a feeling of complete contentment and peace as a result of performing the meditation correctly—it is momentary joy. Naturally, these feelings are subjective and are governed by the meditator's mind. They come in four forms:

   a. Minor rapture

      This is a form of short-duration rapture and is experienced by many meditators. It includes the standing-up of hair strands, the out-pouring of tears, and other minor signs.

   b. Momentary joy

This form takes on a sudden rush of feelings in the meditator's body. These can often be a tingling sensation or a strange current running through your veins. Again, these are just momentary joys and of short duration.

c. Flood of joy

This third form of rapture is again more powerful, but this one does not remain bound by the meditator's feelings. Those who have experienced it have said that it's actually more like rocking your body as if the ground is moving repeatedly.

d. Transporting rapture

This highest level of rapture makes the practitioner light-headed and causes unintentional body movements. Sometimes, the meditator has even levitated off the ground.

4. Bliss

If rapture relates to achieving complete contentment in meditation, bliss (*Sukkha*) is directly concerned with gratification in what the meditator has achieved. However, happiness from a blissful state bears no relation to happiness from worldly or material items. Unlike the momentary joys, a blissful state can last for a very long time.

5. One-pointedness

One-pointedness (*Ekaggata*) is meditative absorption's greatest factor and is achieved only when meditation is performed perfectly. When this occurs, the meditator will experience a sudden feeling of falling deeply somewhere;

this is one-pointedness—the ultimate purpose of meditation. However, some have explained that the meditator must refrain from both being anxious or excited here, because either emotion will disengage the meditator from the level of consciousness required to attain one pointedness. Many meditators fail to experience this level because of the sudden rush of emotions.

The Four Absorptions of Meditation

As mentioned above, while practicing meditation, you will experience and take your mind through these different factors towards peace. The factors above relate to the meditative different absorption levels (*the four Jhanas*), and are used in conjunction with the following four levels of absorption to gauge your state of progress:

1. The First Absorption

    The first absorption (*Patthama Jhana*) is the level of meditation where all five factors of meditative absorption are present.

2. The Second Absorption

    To attain the second absorption (*Dutiya Jhana*) applied thinking and sustained thinking have been mastered, but rapture, bliss, and one-pointedness remain.

3. The Third Absorption

    The third absorption (*Tatiya Jhana*) is attained when rapture is also mastered; the remaining factors of absorption are bliss, and one-pointedness.

4. The Fourth Absorption

When bliss is subdued and mastered, the fourth absorption (*Catuttha Jhana*) is realized, and only equanimity[1] and one-pointedness remain.

---

[1] Equanimity (*Upekkha*) refers to the evenness and unshakeable freedom of mind. It's is self-control, a balanced state-of-mind, strengthened by an absence of strong attachments. In this state, the meditator still notices and cares about events around them, even though they have accepted what is occurring and detached themselves from emotions and feelings.

3

How to Overcome Obstacles in Meditation

There are many distractions before and during meditation. When you appreciate that meditation is a process where we aim to free our thoughts of all mental and physical negative factors, it stands to reason that if we are unable to clear our thoughts and overcome these obstacles, it will be impossible to achieve our goals and desires. Hence, engaging in meditation means that not only do you need to make a serious and concerted effort towards your success, but you also need to understand what obstacles and hindrances you will be faced with, and how best to overcome them. We touched briefly on these hindrances earlier (page 18), but will now cover them in more detail.

Sensory Desire

Sensory desire (*Kamacchanda*) is the craving for sensual fulfillment. It is the desire to please the five senses: sight, smell, taste, hearing, and physical touch, all of which lead to distraction in meditation. For instance, imagine you are in the middle of your practice and you suddenly hear a whistling sound. Your sense of hearing stimulates your brain to open your eyes and locate where the sound is coming from. Eventually, your whole attention is focused on this noise and your thoughts and focus are gone from where they should be—they are lost. This particular hindrance also relates to other forms of desire, such as lust and other means of sexual gratification through touch, sight, or smell. Indeed, gluttony is another factor as your hunger for food incorporates desires to satiate your sense of taste.

To overcome sensory desire, you should acknowledge the presence of the particular desire in question, and then focus on that subject alone. If you acknowledge and convince yourself that this desire does actually exist, instead of giving in and being distracted, you can apply techniques to overcome it.

Some techniques to achieve this include acknowledging and noticing the distraction, and then letting it go. For example, you can take notice of a noise or other distraction and then repeat the distraction in your mind, "The dog is barking, the dog is barking..." and the distraction will eventually disappear. This applies to any sensory desire. Whatever feeling occurs, appears, or touches you, notice it, repeat it in your mind, and it will remove itself.

It is important to remember that our mind is more powerful than all of these desires, and separating ourselves from worldly gratification is a step on the path to experiencing the meditative absorptions (*Jhana*).

Ill Will

Ill will (*Vyapada*) is the desire to dwell on negative strong feelings against other people. As it's not related to the physical senses, but rather to one's emotions or feelings, it is the opposite of sensory desire. Some of these feelings include bitterness, anger, rejection, and a desire to avenge and hurt the person who has harmed you; but, also it's where you hold resentment, regret, and guilt about yourself: ill will is about holding onto unforgiving thoughts.

According to Ajarn Brahmayamso, the remedy to this kind of hindrance is to meditate on the positive feeling of loving kindness (*Metta*). Consequently, instead of fighting with these emotions, rather focus on the feelings themselves and then replace them with compassion and deep sympathy towards daily battles the other person faces. Looking to understand why that particular person hurt you, instead of magnifying their flaws and wrong-doings, is one effective way of redeeming yourself from ill will. Furthermore, it will also lead you towards forgiveness and provide a great opportunity to build a meaningful and loving relationship with others, towards nature, and maybe even to reflect some of it back onto yourself.

Sloth and Torpor

Sloth and torpor (*Thina* and *Middha*), refers to the heaviness of the body and the dullness of the mind, both of which may result in drowsiness during the meditation process. If you are not aware of the initial signs of this hindrance, it will most likely lead you to falling asleep. It is this type of impediment that saps your enthusiasm towards meditation, and drains your energy from concentration, leading you to becoming tired, bored, or both.

To prevent this, before meditating, it is important to have a keen interest in the process as well as a firm goal. This way, you will motivate yourself to achieve your focus and attention. If you do recognize a certain heaviness in your body, or dullness of the mind, then stop for a moment, go for a short walk, or even wash your face to refresh yourself before returning to your meditation. Persisting with the practice while stressing over it is counterproductive.

Restlessness and Worry

Restlessness and worry (*Uddhacca* and *Kukkucca*), refer to the state of mind where the meditator cannot find contentment with anything. It is an anxious attitude driven by a desire to achieve more rather than being satisfied with what you currently have. A prime example is being agitated and then rushing to jump to the next stage of meditation instead of appreciating your presence and achievements in the current process. When this occurs, you're more concerned about how to get to the next level of meditative absorption than you are of doing this level correctly.

Most of us have experienced these obstacles, and the answer is quite simple. These kinds of thoughts lead to total distraction and the best way to overcome such force is to develop an attitude of contentment towards the simple things: be grateful with what you have, instead of magnifying and being concerned with what you don't.

Doubt

Doubt (*Vicikiccha*) refers to the series of unsettling inner questions which occur at a time when you should be moving deeper into silent meditation. Doubt is where you question the ability of a person, the effectiveness of a process, or even interrogate yourself if you have difficulty in producing something positive. Doubt is embracing a building fear inside your heart and mind, rather than embracing the challenge to attain your goal.

You should take clear instruction to overcome doubt in meditation, and learn the necessary procedures correctly. That way, you will develop your confidence in what you do and what you can achieve without any second thoughts. To this end, having a good, trustworthy meditation coach or teacher is a huge aid for a new meditator. The teacher can then nurture you and help build your confidence.

4

Concentration and Meditation Practices

The practice of meditation is extremely important in reducing stress levels and improving focus, as well as developing a strong spiritual connection, regardless of your religious beliefs. This practice has been an essential part of Buddhism and Hinduism, for many years (including yogic practices). There are several different elements and aspects to meditation, including breathing, concentration, and meditation itself; and, you can easily incorporate these traditions into your life to feel both stronger and happier.

Mindfulness of Breathing

Mindfulness of breathing (*Anapanasati*), is a more in-depth focus on the actual breath in meditation—it can also be called breath-based practice. It is an extremely important element in most forms of Buddhism, and has been incorporated into many meditation techniques.

There are many ways to practice mindfulness of breathing, and one of the most common methods is to focus on the breath in cycles of ten-counts. So, the meditator would inhale for a count of ten, then exhale for a count of ten. This creates a rhythm that allows the meditator to focus on their bodily sensations as well as their mental processes. After focusing on the counting, the meditator will then focus on the presence of the breath within the body. They will be aware of the breath as it travels through the nose and the mouth, in through the lungs, and out through the extremities. From there, one can drill-down and focus on the presence of breath as it goes through specific parts of the body. Doing so can improve focus, and can also be used to relax specific muscles or relieve pain. This has been a very important part of Yogic practice.

Traditionally, the practitioner is aware of their natural breath without either forcing or changing it. As part of the practice, they will notice if their breath is short or long, and will make note of it without passing any judgement or changing it. This can be practiced in a sitting position or while standing, and it is recommended that someone new to mindfulness of breathing begins with ten or fifteen minute practice sessions and then work their way up from there.

There are sixteen stages of mindfulness of breathing, and they are divided into four groups (tetrads of stages). Traditionally, and regardless of the level of experience, all meditation sessions should begin with the first stage and work their way through the tetrads.

1. The first tetrad focuses on the body. The meditator first focuses on short and long breaths to gain awareness of their natural rhythms. Then, they will breathe with an awareness

of their entire body in order to separate the breath from the rest of their bodily sensations. Finally, they will focus on tranquillity of the body, in order to reach a state of calmness and relaxation.

2. The second tetrad focuses on feelings. The first stage in this tetrad, is the experience of rapture: connecting the meditator with their feelings, particularly those of inspiration and excitement. From there, in this second tetrad, you move into a state of bliss—a deeper sense of joy. The meditator then lets themselves fully experience these mental activities without change or judgement; and, finally, the meditator tranquilizes their mental state, absorbing these feelings of rapture and bliss.

3. In the third tetrad, the meditator focuses on the heart and mind, primarily by focusing on their positive qualities and energy. Then, they center the mind in a mild state of concentration, which allows the meditator to remain fully involved in their practice. To talk through this process thus far, in the first tetrad, the meditator experienced their mental state; in the second tetrad this expands to gladdening the mind; and now, in the third tetrad, the meditator is able to release their mind, and achieves a wonderful state of liberation.

4. Now the mind has been liberated, the fourth tetrad focuses on the four states of contemplation: impermanence, fading of lust, cessation of involvement, and relinquishment of involvement. At this stage, the meditator will experience the full

benefits of mindfulness of breathing, including peace, insight, freedom, calmness, and centeredness.

Right Concentration

One important form of meditation is right concentration (*Samma Samadhi*). In Buddhism, this is the eighth and final step of the Eightfold Path— the spiritual journey to end suffering. Buddhist monks use right concentration to strengthen their character and other aspects of their lives.

If you remember back to Chapter 2, where we talked about concentration and meditation, those wishing to achieve a state of right concentration must, first, find a space clear of distractions, and then they must find an object on which to concentrate. The basis of this meditation comes from an intense focus on this object. Buddhist meditation manuals suggest different objects which may work more successfully for different personality types.

After the meditator has selected their object, they must then choose a tranquil, distraction-free spot in which to concentrate. The traditional Buddhist meditation position is sitting with legs crossed, with their hands folded in their lap, with good posture through the back, and their eyes closed. Breathing should remain even and full and, by picturing your chosen object and saying the name of that object in your mind, focus should remain fixed. If your mind strays, you should be sure to refocus as quickly as possible, until eventually your mind no longer wanders and your focus is secure. On this path to concentration, as you are likely to encounter many distractions and challenges within your mind, patience is very important.

Once your focus is clear and steady, your mind is free of any distractions, and you have mastered momentary concentration and access concentration—the first two levels of The Threefold Concentration—the meditator can then start to go through absorption concentration—the third And last level of threefold concentration (which is also equivalent to the 1st level of absorption meditation). At this point, the concept of the object will start to become very strong and clear in your mind.

1. The first step, the first absorption (refer to *The Four Absorptions of Meditation*, on page 20), is a state of composure and focus.

2. From there, the mind transitions into the second absorption, which is a state of withdrawal from the physical world, and this creates the states of rapture and pleasure.

3. The third absorption is a state of pleasant, tranquil mindfulness.

4. The fourth absorption is a sort of purity of the mind, where no positive or negative emotions or senses are felt.

As first discussed in section 2.2.2, there are five positive mental factors in Buddhism that will help the meditator through these first four stages: initial focus on the object (applied thinking), retention of focus on the object (sustained thinking), joy and rapture (rapture), happiness (bliss), and unifying the mind (one-pointedness). With these positive mental factors, the daunting task of achieving right concentration is made much easier.

Buddhist monks use these practices for a number of positive reasons: it is said to create wisdom and insight, and to liberate the mind from the troubles of the physical world. The final step on the Eightfold Path to Enlightenment it is a final sense of freedom from suffering, and a transcendence of the distractions of the world.

Again, the concentration practice focuses on oneness with a chosen object which can either be a deliberative or a reflective object. A deliberative object is something physical and perceptible, such as an image of a deity, water or earth, etc. Whereas a reflective object is imperceptible and is more of a concept, such as a chakra, or one's own breathe. After the object has been chosen and focused upon, the meditator can then work towards achieving their goal.

The main task of concentration is to learn to focus the mind on one object without letting distractions creep in. This is extremely challenging and requires significant effort to practice. But, because it can be difficult, the rewards of successful concentration are extremely high; and, one who successfully masters this practice will experience a sense of calm, wisdom, and awareness of both mind and body.

Tranquillity Meditation

Similar to right concentration, the practice of tranquility meditation (*Samatha Panna*), is a Buddhist practice that focuses on soothing the mind and body through concentration on breath. The word *Samatha* means "calm", and *Panna* means "developing wisdom"; and, their main goal is to achieve a sense of calmness through focus on breath in order to develop wisdom. Because the focus on the natural rhythm of one's breath helps simplify thoughts as well as clearing out confusing and distracting stressors, it can help the meditator to feel a sense of clarity in their life. Indeed, true focus on the breath creates a sense of peace, happiness, and oneness with your own body.

The Nine Stages of Mental Abiding

In the practice of tranquility meditation, there are nine stages of training the mind—or "mental abiding"—through which the meditator will be able to access a calm and tranquil mind.

1. The first stage is the placement of the mind. Here, though the meditator focuses on their object of concentration (this is traditionally on the cycle of breath through the torso) they often struggle to maintain that focus. Until they can maintain it, they will remain in the first stage.

2. When the beginner can focus on their breath for about a minute, the second stage of continuous attention has been attained. At this point, the meditator is seeing a drastic improvement and is therefore feeling more motivated with the practice and towards reaching an eventual state of total calm.

3. When the meditator can maintain their focus for almost the entire duration of their practice session, they have reached the third stage of repeated attention. Here they are still aware of distractions, but their increased awareness means they are able to correct it immediately when it happens. The meditator will start to enjoy a real feeling of relaxation, although they are still very far from achieving true calm.

4. The fourth stage of calm attention occurs when the meditator can completely maintain their focus for an hour-long practice session without any distractions. At this point, there are still subtle occurrences of dullness of the mind or excitation.

5. The next stage, tamed attention, occurs when a deep sense of relaxation begins. Often during this stage, the meditator

will mistakenly define mental laxity for calm. This must be avoided as much as possible.

6. The stage of pacified attention occurs only after the meditator has trained consistently for hundreds of hours and has mastered control over occurrences of mental fogginess or laxity. At this point, the awareness of senses and emotions is deeply diminished.

7. Fully pacified attention occurs when instances of mental excitation or dullness are extremely rare. The meditator has a very sharp awareness of these elements and can correct them immediately. At this point, the meditator can focus for several hours at a time.

8. The eight stage is single-pointed attention, and occurs when this strong meditative state can be reached with ease.

9. The final stage to tranquillity meditation is attentional balance, and occurs when the meditator can focus for hours at a time with complete ease and no distractions.

After reaching the 9th, final, stage of calmness, the meditator can start to proceed with the 1st of the 4 levels of meditative absorption (*the 4 jhanas*).

From this state of calmness, the meditator will feel a sense of great lightness and openness. It is from here that they can proceed onto the intense focus of concentration. The focus on breath and calm through the body that has been achieved here is also extremely beneficial to one's physical health, because it rids the body of unnecessary tension that can cause health problems.

Insight Meditation

While tranquility meditation focuses on calmness, the meditation practice of insight meditation or Vipassana Panna focuses on developing a sense of thoughtfulness about the world. This style of meditation has become very popular in the Western world and is known as "mindfulness meditation". The word Vipassana means "to see things as they really are", and Panna means "developing wisdom". Thus, these forms of meditation focus on clarity of the mind during which the Three Characteristics are discovered and contemplated: impermanence, suffering, and non-self awareness (emptiness). They are considered the three most important insights into the true nature of reality. This is a very introspective meditation practice and, as such, has become a popular way of processing difficult emotional situations.

As mentioned in Chapter 2.2.3, there are four meditative absorptions in insight meditation: the first stage/first absorption, is an exploration of mind and body where the meditator focuses on how they affect each other. In the second absorption, the trials of the first stage slowly dissipate, and the practice begins to feel effortless; feelings of rapture, joy, and bliss are common in this stage. In the third absorption, these feelings leave, and a sense of true happiness and tranquility is left. Finally, the fourth absorption is characterized by a unity of the mind and openness to knowledge and wisdom.

Like tranquility meditation, insight meditation also focuses on the mindfulness of breathing. However, instead of focusing on it in a way that creates complete calm, insight meditation focuses on the breath as a catalyst for introspection. The main goal is to gain insight into the true nature of reality. Impermanence is a very important concept here because it emphasizes how changeable and fragile life is. The meditator is encouraged to notice these things and, due to the ever-changing nature of the universe and because our pain and suffering is insubstantial and will change, to then let them go.

Insight meditation is traditionally done in a place of calm, such as a forest or under a tree (if you can get that close to nature); but any quiet place should suffice. The posture here is the same as in right concentration and tranquility meditation, sitting with legs crossed and an upright back. Here your focus is on the rise and fall of your breath. However, unlike these previous methods, for insight meditation, interruptions or distractions should be noted, and again let go. Choosing simple words to note experiences and mental objects is best, as they can be incorporated into the rhythm of the breath. After a session of insight meditation, this practice can be carried over into one's daily activities.

Daily Meditation Practices

Now we've come this far, the question is how do we incorporate these complicated practices into our everyday life? Well, the easiest way is to set aside a manageable amount of time every day to dedicate to meditation practice, 10 minutes will do to start. It is best to meditate at the same time every day because that will help turn this new practice into a habit. Furthermore, it is also a good idea to set aside a specific quiet space for your meditation; and, when you start, make sure you are suitably clothed and in a comfortable position that you will be able to maintain—remember, the main goal in the beginning is to focus your mind.

If you haven't skipped chapters to come to this page, you now realize that lack of focus is the most common problem for beginners, so it helps to pick a really strong image to focus on at first. Focusing on your breath works really well for many people, and is a principle reason why breath-based practice or mindfulness of breathing is so popular all over the world. If you prefer, you can also stare at an image or an object: many find that lighting a candle is both an aid to focus, as well helping to create a mood conducive to meditation.

When you start, try to remove your mind from yourself. Observe your body's sensations and feelings, but don't let yourself be present in these feelings. Imagine you are a person outside of your body looking down from above, and calmly watching yourself. This does take a bit of practice, and it will probably help you to find guided meditation to follow; but, there are many recordings on the Internet that are perfect for just this. They can be found through YouTube, podcasts on iTunes, or just a simple Google search.

Once you have mastered mindfulness of breathing, you can try focusing your breath through different parts of your body. Some people start at the head and work down to the feet, or vice versa. If you do have trouble calming your mind this may actually help you, as instead of trying to empty your mind completely on the first try, it gives you something to focus on while you are meditating.

I hope you realize that these are just basic steps towards an eventual bigger meditation goal of right concentration, tranquility meditation, and insight meditation; and all these practices can be performed through mindfulness of breathing. What is important is you take your time, and you work through the steps as slowly and as thoroughly as you need to, to enable you to have a quality and meaningful meditation experience. These states of concentration, calm, and insight will never be mastered overnight (and many spend their entire lives working towards mastery); but you can and will see very fast initial results. Within a very short time of working through the steps, you will most likely see an improvement in both your mental state and your physical health, which will help enormously in motivating you to continue towards your goal.

Finally, the wide variety of meditation styles make them applicable to people from all walks of life; so, no matter your culture, age, career, or circumstance, you can benefit from meditation. Whether it's just a simple, daily 5 minute breathing exercise, or a dedicated study of right concentration, you will develop your sense of self, your understanding of the world, and your health.

Author's Page

Duangta Wanthong Mondi is Thai and a Buddhist. She lives and works in the North-east of Thailand as an English teacher in a Thai State school.

Duangta has an M. Ed. In Teaching English as a Foreign Language (TEFL), and has co-authored a series of books to help English speakers learn Thai.

The series is called *Quest (**Qu***ick, **E**asy, ***S**imple **T**hai)* and consists of:

- *Learning Thai, Your Great Adventure*

- *Learn Thai Alphabet with Memory Aids to Your Great Adventure*

- *The Perfect Thai Phrasebook*

- *How to Read Thai*

- *The Learn Thai Alphabet application* (web and iPad app)

- *The Learn Thai Numbers application* (web and iPad app)

Website – *http://www.teachermondi.com*

Facebook - *https://www.facebook.com/teachermondi*

A Beginner's Guide to Buddhism

Check out my recent book '*A Beginner's Guide to Buddhism*'. Available from my website at http://www.teachermondi.com or Amazon.

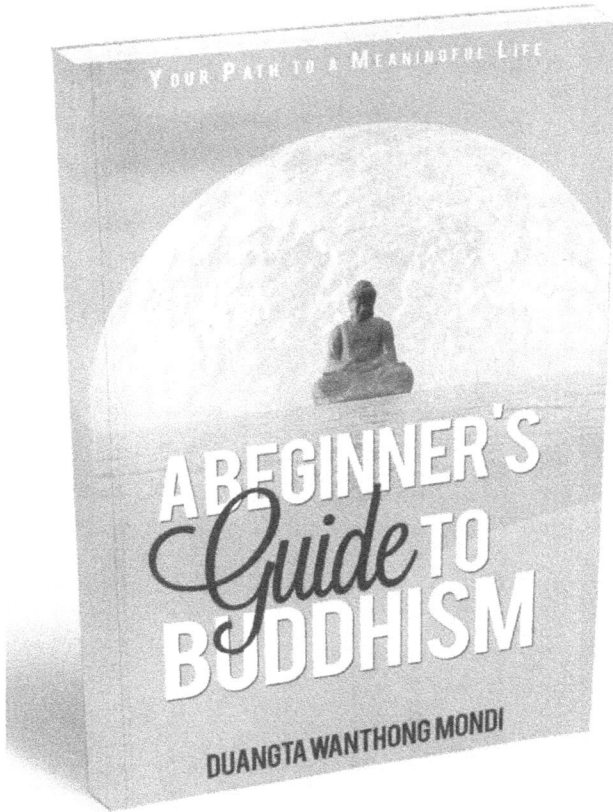

Check out my author page on Amazon.

amazon.com/author/duangtamondi